Garfield County Libraries
Silt Branch Library
680 Home Avenue
Silt, CO 81652
(970) 876-5500 • Fax (970) 876-5921
www.GCPLD.org

PET CARE LIBRARY

Caring for Your Parakeet

by Colleen Sexton

BELLWETHER MEDIA • MINNEAPOLIS, MN

BLASTOFF! READERS 4

Note to Librarians, Teachers, and Parents:

Blastoff! Readers are carefully developed by literacy experts and combine standards-based content with developmentally appropriate text.

Level 1 provides the most support through repetition of high-frequency words, light text, predictable sentence patterns, and strong visual support.

Level 2 offers early readers a bit more challenge through varied simple sentences, increased text load, and less repetition of high-frequency words.

Level 3 advances early-fluent readers toward fluency through increased text and concept load, less reliance on visuals, longer sentences, and more literary language.

Level 4 builds reading stamina by providing more text per page, increased use of punctuation, greater variation in sentence patterns, and increasingly challenging vocabulary.

Level 5 encourages children to move from "learning to read" to "reading to learn" by providing even more text, varied writing styles, and less familiar topics.

Whichever book is right for your reader, Blastoff! Readers are the perfect books to build confidence and encourage a love of reading that will last a lifetime!

This edition first published in 2011 by Bellwether Media, Inc.

No part of this publication may be reproduced in whole or in part without written permission of the publisher. For information regarding permission, write to Bellwether Media, Inc., Attention: Permissions Department, 5357 Penn Avenue South, Minneapolis, MN 55419.

Library of Congress Cataloging-in-Publication Data
Sexton, Colleen.
Caring for your parakeet / by Colleen Sexton.
  p. cm. – (Blastoff! readers. Pet care library)
Summary: "Developed by literacy experts for students in grades two through five, this title provides readers with basic information for taking care of parakeets"–Provided by publisher.
 Includes bibliographical references and index.
 ISBN 978-1-60014-470-7 (hardcover : alk. paper)
1. Budgerigar–Juvenile literature. I. Title.
SF473.B8S39 2010
636.6'865–dc22   2010011479

Printed in the United States of America, North Mankato, MN.
080110   1162

Contents

Choosing Parakeets

! fun fact

Parakeets are also called budgies.

Parakeets are some of the most popular pets in the world! These little birds are clever and friendly.

Before you go to a pet store, take time to learn about parakeets to be sure they are the right pets for you. They live for 10 to 15 years. They need to be cared for every day. You will also need supplies from the pet store to care for them.

cage

Supply List

Here is a list of supplies you will need to take care of parakeets.

- cage
- perches
- food cups
- dry and wet food
- water bottle
- cuttlebone
- blanket
- parakeet toys

dry food

cuttlebone

fun fact

Parakeets come in hundreds of color combinations!

Parakeets are social birds. It is best to get at least two birds. They will keep each other from getting lonely when you are not around.

If you can, bring your parakeets home when they are young. Four months is a good age. Young parakeets adjust to a new home more easily than older birds.

Setting Up a Parakeet Cage

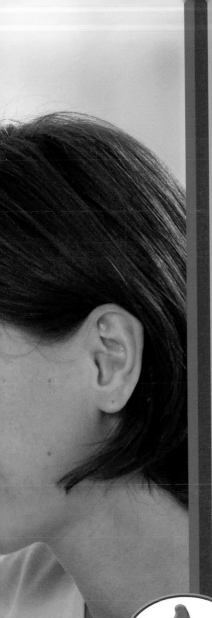

Your parakeets need a place to live. Set up a cage that has plenty of room for flying. Put the cage in a room where people spend a lot of time.

The cage should have bars that are close together. This will keep your parakeets from getting stuck between bars or escaping. The bars are also good for climbing.

Care Tip

Never put a parakeet's cage in the kitchen. The cooking smells can be dangerous for birds.

Set up **perches** for your parakeets to sit on. Choose two or three perches of different thicknesses. Place them at different heights inside the cage.

perch

dry food cup

Hang two food cups inside the cage near the perches. Use one for dry food and one for wet food. You also need to provide a water bottle. Always keep it full of fresh, clean water.

Feeding Your Parakeets

Care Tip

A parakeet's beak never stops growing. Pecking a cuttlebone helps a parakeet keep its beak a healthy length.

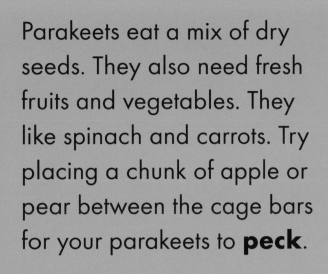

Parakeets eat a mix of dry seeds. They also need fresh fruits and vegetables. They like spinach and carrots. Try placing a chunk of apple or pear between the cage bars for your parakeets to **peck**.

Give your parakeets a **cuttlebone** to peck for extra **nutrients**. You can also buy parakeet treats at a pet store.

cuttlebone

Health and Exercise

A clean cage is important to the health of your parakeets. Wash their food cups and water bottle every day. Line the bottom of the cage with newspaper and change it every day. Wash the whole cage once a week.

Parakeets like baths! They will splash around in a shallow dish of water. They will also rub themselves clean with wet lettuce leaves.

fun fact
Parakeets lose feathers that are old and worn. New feathers grow in their places.

Check your parakeets every day for changes in their health. Sick birds might be quieter or less active. They might also eat less. Take your parakeets to a **veterinarian** if you see these signs.

Parakeets need exercise to stay healthy. Let them out of the cage to fly as often as you can. Make sure all the doors and windows in your home are closed!

Parakeets like **routine**. Most parakeets are active in the morning and afternoon. They take a nap in the middle of the day. They also like to eat at the same times every day.

Parakeets need 10 to 12 hours of sleep a day. Cover the cage with a blanket at night to block light. Uncover the cage at the same time each morning.

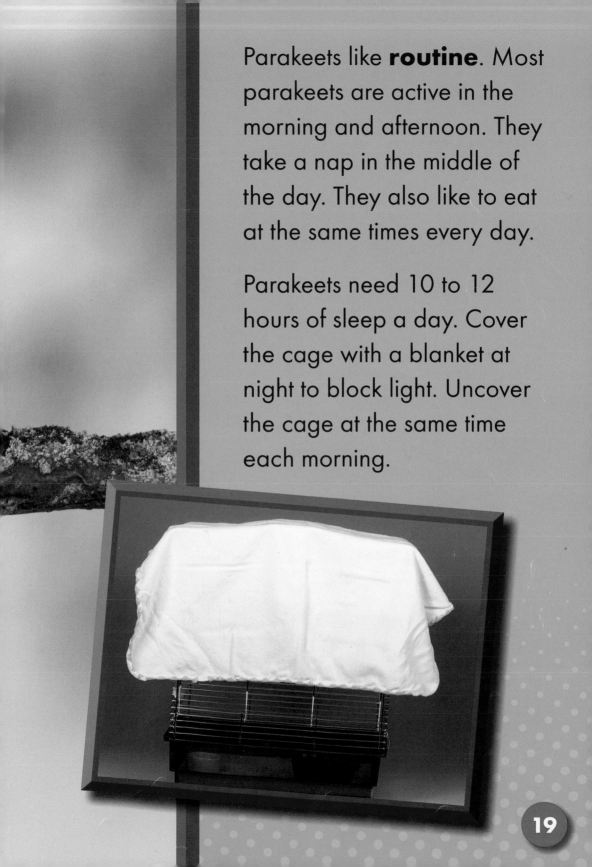

Playing and Training

! fun fact

You can train your parakeets to perch on your finger or sit in your hand.

Parakeets like to play. Keep many different toys around and give your parakeets a few at a time. Swings and balls are great toys for parakeets.

Parakeets chirp and chatter. Some can **mimic** sounds like a ringing phone or a creaking door. You might even be able to train your parakeets to talk!

Glossary

cuttlebone–part of a cuttlefish; cuttlebones have calcium to keep a parakeet's bones, heart, and muscles healthy.

mimic–to copy the action, speech, or sound of something else

nutrients–substances plants and animals need to stay healthy; nutrients come from food and other sources.

peck–to take food bit by bit with a beak

perches–horizontal rods on which a bird sits; parakeets and other birds hold on to perches with their claws.

routine–a regular way of doing something; parakeets like to eat, sleep, and exercise at the same times every day.

veterinarian–a doctor who takes care of animals

To Learn More

AT THE LIBRARY
Birmelin, Immanuel. *My Parakeet and Me.*
Hauppauge, N.Y.: Barron's Educational, 2001.

Mataya, Marybeth. *Are You My Bird?* Edina, Minn.:
Magic Wagon, 2009.

Stevens, Kathryn. *Parakeets*. Mankato, Minn.:
The Child's World, 2009.

ON THE WEB
Learning more about pet care
is as easy as 1, 2, 3.

1. Go to www.factsurfer.com.

2. Enter "pet care" into the search box.

3. Click the "Surf" button and you will see a list of
   related Web sites.

With factsurfer.com, finding more information is just a
click away.

Index

The images in this book are reproduced through the courtesy of: Juan Martinez, front cover, p. 5 (top, middle); Juniors Bildarchiv/Photolibrary, front cover (small), pp. 4-5, 5 (bottom), 8-9, 12-13, 13 (small), 16-17, 21 (small); Juniors Bildarchiv/Age Fotostock, pp. 6-7, 15, 18-19, 19 (small); Rob Byron, p. 10; Sarycheva Olesia, p. 11; fotototo/Age Fotostock, p. 14; Image100 Limited/Photolibrary, p. 16 (small); blickwinkel/Alamy, pp. 20-21.